He Spoke

To Me

He Spoke

To Me

by

Patricia A. Golden

Cradle Press
P.O. Box 8401
St. Louis, MO 63132

First edition 2018

Library of Congress Catalog-in-Publication-Data

He Spoke To Me / Patricia A. Golden – 1st ed.

Golden, Patricia A. (March, 2017)

Book design by Michael Golden

Cover art and concept by Michael A. Golden

Graphic design by Ryan Francisco

Library of Congress Control Number: 2018946983

Paperback ISBN 978-0-9979537-2-5

"For me, prayer is an aspiration of the heart,

it is a simple glance directed to heaven,

it is a cry of gratitude and love in the midst

of trial as well as joy; finally it is something

great, supernatural, which expands my soul

and unites me to Jesus."

Therese de Lisieux

Introduction

My name is Pat Golden, originally from Chicago, where my husband Warren and I raised our five children.

In the fall of 1978, my husband's job transferred him to Houston, where we lived for three years before moving to St. Louis in the spring of 1981. We always thought we'd return to Chicago, but loved St. Louis and stayed.

I think it may be important for you to understand how the words in this book came about. I usually began my prayer time alone praising God and talking to Him, gradually becoming quiet to listen. On April 13, 1980, I was having this quiet time and experienced a great peace come upon me. I knew this was special and our Lord had some words for me. I had a small tablet of paper with me and I pulled it out. I closed my eyes and became aware of seeing words scrolling across in my mind and I was aware that they were from our Lord or the Holy Spirit. I was amazed; it seemed very normal. I had no fear or illusion that it was real, and began to hear His words.

It was His first visit.

One time, the words even appeared as if on a ticker tape scrolling past my field of vision. It struck me as though the Lord had a sense of humor, since I was so familiar with numbers from my love of math.

I would open my eyes occasionally to quickly write down the words. I often used shorthand, a skill I had learned years earlier, because I didn't want to miss anything I was seeing or hearing. It was as if I had been prepared for these experiences, which helped me not to be frightened. Later, I would write or type each word of the messages from the notes in my pad.

Over the years it was the Lord who chose the times and places. Sometimes when I knew the Lord was about to speak to me, I would find a place for quiet and listen to Him. There are times He still speaks to me by seeing words go by. Sometimes shorter messages come as if I hear Him speaking the words to me.

Some of the words were just for me, but many of the words were meant to be shared. For many years, I lacked the courage to share much because I didn't think anyone would believe me. After several years, and finally sharing some of the writings at Prayer Meetings, I found that others were also touched and felt personal connections to these words. People loved them.

This book, *He Spoke To Me*, contains some of the messages I have been given over many years. Besides the prophecies in this book, I have also received what I consider to be meditations and teachings.

I believe that through my mind and soul I accepted this as a gift from the Holy Spirit. Now I humbly pass this gift on to you. My hope is that each of you finds words in the following pages as if He was speaking to you, personally.

Acknowledgements

I would like to thank the following people on the occasion of putting this book together:

My husband Warren for supporting me throughout the years in my endeavors and I believe he was with me encouraging me, as he knew others would receive grace.

My son Michael for giving me the strength not to give up. With his help I have been able to persevere and see these words in print.

My sister Catherine for gifting me with her editing skills.

Linda Borchardt, who early on suggested I publish this work. She saw the possibilities that I had yet to see.

Chris Franke, who helped me early on with filing and typing and for a final glance before printing.

Be A People of Love

I want you to pray with my people and teach

my people the ways of the Spirit,

and I want my people to know my Voice and

walk in my ways.

I want a strong people. I am raising up my

shepherds to

care for their brothers and sisters

who are struggling to find my Kingdom.

They will recognize me by my Peace

that you bring to them.

Open the doors wide and be a People of Love.

As you grow in love and as you grow in the

knowledge

of me, I will draw into your midst

the broken – those in turmoil, the lonely, those in

darkness.

Receive them well and they shall have their fill as

they are

drawn into my Peace and Love. I love you.

April 13, 1980

Seek the Lordship of God

You, yes You, I love you.
And I speak to each of you by name.
Fear not for I am with you.
Do not be afraid to cross over that bridge, to come
through the darkness of a tunnel, to cross around to
the other side of the mountain, for I am with you,
and behind you, guiding you on the path, for I am
the direct route to my Father, the Creator of all
things.
Be not afraid for together we come through the
darkness and into the warmth and living Presence
of my Father Who surrounds His Heavenly
creatures and the Communion of Saints, yet is the
object of their worship. I challenge you to come
into the darkness and through that darkness and be
lifted up into the Holy of Holies, into the Cleft of the
Rock, into the Rejoicing and Joy in Heavenly
Places.
Seek the Lordship of your God above all else.
Come and worship the Godhead. Bow down in your
spirit, my children, so that you will know it is your
Father Who lifts you high. It is also He who raises
up the Lowly.
Be still, my little ones, and abide in your Lord.

14

Remember, my children, it is the Resurrection
Power that enables you to be at the right hand of
my Father with me.

Seek repentance, my children. Ask and you shall
receive forgiveness.

The Godhead knows the condition of each heart.

Come and enter more fully into that which you are
created for.

Remember, you lack everything. I lack nothing.

You are powerless. The spirit of God is all
Powerful.

You do not know all things in my spiritual world. I
am All Knowing.

You become confused and lose your direction. I am
All Wisdom.

You become impatient with one another and with
one's self and too often compete with one another
and with one's self. I am Perfect Love.

You are so frail, my children, and I am All Strength.

Your earthly teachers lack what the Perfect
Rabboni can teach you.

Abide in Me. Live in Me. Walk in My Ways. Listen
to Me.

Absorb in some measure the many-faceted
attributes of your God.

Be filled with the Spirit of God and reflect His Peace and His Love.

You are dear to Me, and I encourage you on to greatness.

November 12, 1981

On The Road

Peace be with you. Blessed are you who are like
little children. Know that I love you, my beloved.
How I cherish you when you are with one another
and share the deeper things of my Kingdom.

It was like that on the road to Emmaus. The walk
that day was not so different from your day's walk.
Share your life with one another. Walk with each
other. Speak the questions in your heart to one
another. Remember, I am on the road with you. So
often you struggle and question.

Be at peace, my children on the road. My grace is
sufficient for you to see me. Look to the right and to
the left. Do you not perceive me? For behold, I am
there. I rejoice in you, my children of the Kingdom!
It is I Who gives you the grace to persevere and
overcome hurdles. It is I Who walks on the road
daily with you and Who wipes the sweat from your
brow, washes the dirt from your feet and gives you
new life to quench the dryness from the walk.

Be wise as serpents, my fellow travelers. Keep
alive your life in me and you shall recognize me

more often on the road. Listen to the prophets, children of the Kingdom. My prophets are moving among my people today just as there were prophets of old. Those who heeded the prophets of old recognized me as Lord and Savior. They were surprised by nothing—from my birth to Gethsemane to Calvary.

Be filled with my Spirit. Be filled with my Wisdom. Be filled with my Love. Fear no man. Look to no man. For I am your Lord, your Friend, your Fellow Traveler, your Lover.

Go and bear witness to my Birth, Death and Resurrection. I love you and treasure you.

February 23, 1982

A City of Hope

Yes, it is true I called you for my glory. I have brought many from the north and from the south, from the east and from the west to build a City of Hope. It is MY desire that I have put into your heart to build a new Jerusalem to deliver my people, to feed my people, to love as I would love my people.

I've taken you through a time of yearning, confusion, aloneness so you could see more clearly the state of my church.
My people should be a people of joy.
My people should be victorious over evil.
My people should be breaking down the walls isolating them from relationships with their brothers and sisters.
My people are comparing and measuring their spirituality with one another rather than with me, their Lord.

Oh, how I weep for my people. It would be so easy if they would seek me, turn to me, come to my Father, be filled with My Spirit, be nourished by our Love, be brought into unity by Our Oneness, be healed by the Oils of the Holy Spirit of God.

Then my church shall rise up and all of my chosen people from far and near shall become visible in the most powerful witness the world has ever seen acclaiming the Father, Son and Holy Spirit.

Sometime in 1983

I Have Chosen You

I was praying in the Spirit and began to see myself above the earth looking at the world rotating. It was a black, scorched earth, but I could see many bonfires – small to large as the world rotated. I knew that they represented groups of Christians praying. I asked the Holy Spirit what this meant and heard the following words.

I have chosen you and in your need you have responded and sought after me. There are many like you in the Body of Christ whom I am strengthening and purifying for a great spiritual harvest. My church has been laid waste; my people have been in desolation for lack of knowing me and my Word. Come away with me, my beloved, and see my church – for as far as you can see, it is in ruins, not what my Father planned for His sons and daughters. See how the locust has eaten away; see how the spirit of the world has deceived so many; see the shepherds who did not feed my people milk and honey.

But I show you this to fill you with Hope, to tell you, my daughter (son) that my Father is creating anew His Church – something you cannot imagine – already the seeds are sown; there is much nurturing and watering going on.

See how my spirit-filled disciples are moving out into the wasteland. Soon there will be a harvest, but just now there is much tenderness in an infant, spirit-filled church. I call you to be sent forth in this wasteland to bring my love, my healing, my strengthening, my protection until one by one my people stand tall before me empowered with my Spirit – and you shall see those working in the wasteland multiply rapidly, and my Church will be renewed and my people will be strengthened to glorify the Father, Son and Holy Spirit in all things.

October 19, 1983

I Will Listen To You

My child, come to me often in the depths of quiet prayer – childlike.

Put your hand in mine and speak with me – of your needs and what you fear most. Let me take your hand and fill you with Peace. Do not be afraid. Let my Love and concern touch your spirit. I will listen to you. And know, my special friend, I understand. It is important that you learn to trust me and to listen to me when we come together in quiet. You must let your faith grow and deepen as time goes by for I am at work in your life for your good and those you love.

Look to me for faith, guidance, direction and strength. Be obedient to that inner voice and trust that it is I. If your heart is right, my Spirit will protect you. Worship my Father. Seek after the Kingdom. Be a witness of obedience to my Father as I was. Blest are you for responding to grace.

October 6, 1986

Shepherd My People

I am forming a precious jewel and each of you is a facet of this gem.

You, my beloved, are a remnant people. You have responded to my grace with a generous heart and spirit.

Be not afraid for I will be your strength, courage and fortitude.

Support one another in the unity of the Trinity – Father, Son and Spirit.

Drink from the water of Life for I pour it out in abundance to my people who are willing to receive.

Shepherd my people whom I send into your lives for I am constantly searching out those of my beloved who are in great need. Be Me for them.

Believe that I walk among you and touch you –
faith is yours.

What is it that you need? Speak it to me. Come to
me often to be filled and nurtured and healed.

Look to Wisdom – seek after discernment. Follow
in my ways. Listen to your brothers and sisters.
Never be too proud to be centered in me. I will
give you the gifts needed to stand firm against the
adversaries of the world. I will bless you with the
oils of my spirit in the name of the Father, Son and
Holy Spirit.

I anoint you to go forth in my name.

late 1980's

Shoreline of the Sea of Galilee

A hand was leading me to water.

"Come to the water and be filled with my blessings

I will put a great thirst in you for me

Seek forgiveness of your sins

Seek me to be filled with my Love

Speak to me of your needs

I am listening

You don't even have to touch the hem of my

garment to be healed and made whole

I know your thoughts, desires and dreams

Turn to me so you will know it is I who lives in you

Bear witness to my love for you"

May 28, 1999

You Will be Blest

Plant your feet firmly in my prints.
Come follow Me –
Know My voice. I will lead you to places you could
never go alone.
I will carry a torch to light the way.

He touches our heart with the torch. I will inflame
your hearts to know me and follow me.
I have much to teach you.
Be filled with my Spirit.

He touches our head with the torch. I will enlighten
you with the things of my Kingdom.

*He touches our hands, feet and our side with the
torch.*
To follow me will not always be easy, but I am with
you.

My peace is with you.
My love is with you.

Be still and listen for it.

Come, follow me.

You will be blessed.

Bring my Life to those whose paths we cross.

I will be with you.

You are mine. I love and bless you.

Come!

September 16, 1999

Know That I Am Near

See yourself as the woman washing Jesus' feet with

oil.

Come into my presence and be lifted up

I will fill you with joy

Come, take my hand

Come into my heart

Be one with Me

Become childlike and you shall see Me in your joys

and trials

Know that I am near and dwell in you

I am your strength and courage

I nudge you to come closer

I anoint you and desire to make you whole.

August 16, 2000

Open Ourself to Grace

In my spirit I sense our Lord placing the sign of the cross upon each of us.

Our Lord calls forth each of us and claims us as His own.

He is pouring out great grace in our lives to open ourselves to Him to receive healing in areas of ourselves that would prevent us from receiving Him more fully.

There is joy in heaven when each of us responds to grace – we open ourselves and make ourselves vulnerable.

September 13, 2000

Come Into My Heart

I gave my Life for you

I breathed my Spirit upon you

Come into my Heart

I invite you to become one with me

I draw all men unto myself

It is my desire to bring my healing love to you

So that you may become all that I created you to

be

I see the beauty in you

Turn to me, come to me, seek me

I will set you free so that the beauty in you may

unfold

I embrace you and am with you

May, 2001

The Glow From Within Us

The Holy Spirit tells us, "The dark days are already here. There will be many attacks by the evil one against you and against my Kingdom. You will walk in darkness but the devil will not deter you from the path nor overtake you."

Jesus tells us, "You are covered in the Blood of the Lamb. You are covered in the greatest of all Treasures – ME. Jesus.

And as you walk even through these dark times, the glow from within you will light your path and it will light the path for many others.

Go in Peace and be in Peace. My Spirit is within you and my Kingdom will have no end."

May, 2001

I Am Speaking

Turn to Me to receive the abundant life.

It is my desire to fill my people with my Spirit.

I am speaking.

You must be still and listen to hear my voice.

Open your heart to my Spirit and I will fill you with

love.

Come to me.

Put your hand in Mine.

Let Me embrace and hold you.

I will heal your soul.

August 1, 2001

Turn To Me

Turn to Me
Let me fill your heart with my peace
Turn to me for guidance in your life
Embrace one another
Open your hearts to my gifts so that you will
be strengthened and bless my people in my name
The heavens will open and my grace will pour out
on you
You are not alone
I am with you
Lean on Me
Seek Me

September 9, 2001

Stand Before Me

Do not hide your face from me

Rise up

Stand before me

My light shall fall upon you

My unconditional love will purify you

You will know your God lives

Raise your spirit and rejoice in Me

Look to Me for your wholeness

Be joyful that you are my child

Rejoice in Me

May 13, 2002

Who Will Bring the Light to Them?

I was at great Peace sitting in a small chapel during Adoration of the Blessed Sacrament. I was the only one there. I can look out at trees and I am reminded of a cabin in the woods I would go to. God is blessing me <u>very</u> deeply. Suddenly the Holy Spirit began speaking and showing me the following:

"The world is spiraling around faster and faster in the wrong direction. Not upward toward Me.
Look closely at the string around it.
There are people tied together out of control.
They are headed toward darkness.
Do they not see I am up here in the Light?
I can free any one of those people who want to detach from the rest.
Pray for Grace to be received by them – those who are ready.
Many are looking for Me, but who will bring the Light to them?"

"You take it too lightly when my Mother says, 'Pray and fast.' Heed her words! The darkness is near. Prepare yourself."

I respond, "God forgive me my sins, any self-righteousness, any neglect of my time with You, and my judgment of others."

I see an image of a Dove over me with a Host just beneath its claws. It changes to an altar and I see large, bright, red drops of Blood. Jesus is at the altar holding up a Chalice and Host. Around Him are angels and off to the left, among them is, I believe, Mary – letting me know to follow her.

Then, suddenly, I see Archangel Michael on a huge white horse. I understand that Michael is readying an army. He was on a high ridge and below in a protected environment, but not a valley, were people gathering, but not many. I know that these people will be prepared to follow Him in a spiritual war. It will be a small army compared to the number of people in the world.

Michael is holding a large sword in one hand and in the other he is holding a long staff. It touched the ground and went high above him. The staff and the cloth over the horse where St. Michael sat is made of stunning colors: some white but mostly shades of blue, less than navy and slightly darker than royal blue, and also exquisite ruby red and gold.

He is just sitting there in the image, waiting while more gather to form his army.

I was at great peace and the image was over and I got up, but then thought to ask our Lord for some sort of confirmation and I waited.

Suddenly Nehemiah 4 came into my spirit. I was not familiar with it, so I read the whole chapter and the following is what caught my spirit:

- Keep doing our work and stand guard
- Become workers in the field and prayer warriors and warnings

- Have no fear
- Fight for your brother, etc.
- Trumpeter warns us when danger is near and we must pick up the slack
- Work is scattered (I recalled the vision of the scorched earth and bonfires of all sizes)
- God will fight with us
- Some will be praying as workers need protection

January 27, 2005

"My dear one, I will never leave you."

He takes me as a child and gives me new shoes, and takes me by the hand and tells me that He will take me places I would never go on my own.

I follow His path and He opens my world to things I never thought possible.

"I adore thee, oh Christ, and I praise You because by your Holy Cross You have redeemed the world."

He tells me, "Sit with me and learn from me. This is a time of preparation, discipline and listening. We will pause while you grow in these lessons. Come here (on the path) often where I will teach you. I love you. I am preparing you."

"I need to remember that You have given me a new pair of shoes for my new path with You, and You will help and protect me on this journey. Please keep my heart open to Your Graces. I have to remind myself that I don't need to know what you are preparing me for."

"OPEN YOUR HANDS TO RECEIVE ALL THAT MY FATHER HAS FOR YOU."

January 2005

Focus On the Gift of the Holy Spirit

Imagine being on the deck of a cabin surrounded by trees and birds singing. It is so peaceful you don't want to move. Thank you, Lord, for this place. There is a small hill down to the dirt road below. I see you coming up the hill, Lord, to visit me. Thank you for bringing me to this place.

I know You are here and I know when You have to go. Your Presence will linger on. It is your desire to have prepared this place in my heart to meet me today. I want to listen to hear your Will for me more clearly. "First of all, remember to ask. Focus on the Gift of the Holy Spirit and all He desires to bring to you."

Lord, I must find 'the place' at home for my quiet time and awareness of your Presence – a special place. "Come to Me often to be restored – there is work to be accomplished.

Can You tell me what that is? "Not yet. I am preparing all of you for it." He will help me to be

41

more fervent in finding my quiet time and place at home.

I realize I do not ask your Will as often as I should. "I will teach you how...and remind you. I want you to sit with me awhile now."

Lord, I struggle with how to use my time. "Yes, I know. You have discernment to know this weakness." Lord, I blame it on my age, the need to finish a project, multi-tasking, excuses. "Recapture the order you need in your life. You have it and are not using it wisely. You already know how to solve this and set time aside." Lord, I'll work on this and come back to You. "Learn to stop doing trivial things and think through what is most important and put things in order of priority. Time spent with me is of utmost importance."

May, 2007

Patience

"...I have been preparing your heart. Together, with many, My Temple is being restored. This is a work you will know in your spirit and does not have to be shouted about. I will draw you closer and closer to my Heart and my Mother. Listen to Me, I will direct you in the restoration of my Temple.   Be patient."

January 4, 2007

Gentleness

I asked, "Did You really send an angel to the Group?" "I did indeed send a special angel to protect your group."

I asked her name again, and a response followed immediately.

Gentleness like a soft breeze blowing over a field of
     red flowers.
Gentleness like the tall grass swaying in the
     sunlight.
Gentleness like a child's love.
Gentleness like a caress.
Gentleness like a soft mist on your face.
Gentleness like my Mother.
Gentleness is her name.
Gentleness is graceful.
Gentleness moves softly over the field of red
     flowers as though they were a field of your
     hearts.

June 24, 2007

Holiness

"Just be a good person and listen to my Father

teach you

Sit in His Presence

Open your heart and will to His living in you

Allow His Love and Light to penetrate you

I will hold your hand and walk with you

You will be safe

Holiness is living a simple life remembering to be

aware of My Life in you

My Sprit will move in you

Do not be afraid"

June 19, 2008

Road to Emmaus

As I begin to pray, I have strong feelings; a desire to change, too much stress. What is Jesus saying to me?

Holy Spirit: "Follow Me to the water *(I was carrying chairs and put them down)*. Do not burden yourself. Come by yourself and rest with me; come into the water and be refreshed. Trust Me. I know where I am taking you. Again, rest in Me – quiet yourself. Trust Me to let you know where we are going."

November 5, 2008

The Living Waters

During a time of quiet, I saw in my spirit an avalanche or raging waters tumbling down a hillside, which may or may not have been destructive.

The avalanche or raging waters do not resemble God's living waters. In my mind they represent Satan's rage raining down on humanity to devour us...to reign havoc on God's Kingdom here on earth.

God's waters are calm and blessed; healing and full of grace. They cleanse us of sin and give us new life; they do not destroy us as promised in the days of Noah. (Gen 8:21 and 9:12-16)

I believe the raging waters are a sign of Satan and not of God, although He allows it. Mankind is turning away from God to self. The world is in distress.

God is calling us to pray for His Mercy on America and the World; pray that souls will turn to Him and ask for Mercy, especially those who call themselves Christian and walk in darkness or their own light. God wants to reclaim the land for Himself.
(Genesis 9:21)

(Also see: Jeremiah 16:11-12, 16:16-17, 17:5-10, 12-13, 18:6-10)

1 John 1:5-10 "Here, then is the message we have heard from Him and announce to you; that God is light; in him there is no darkness."

November 17, 2008

Help Me See And Hear You

Luke 1:35 The Holy Spirit will come upon you and
the power of the Most High will overshadow you.
Luke 1:38 Mary said, "I am the servant of the Lord.
Let it be done to me as you say."

"At this Advent season dear Father, we ask for a
new birth, deeper than any we've ever
experienced, of your Son, Jesus. Help me enter a
new depth of my life in Christ with the healing I
need to see You, to hear You, to witness to Your
life in me."

"Touch me to the depths of my soul with Your
precious blood and enable me to have a renewed
and deeper relationship with my Father, His Son
Jesus and the Holy Spirit. Help me to shed my own
selfish dreams and habits so I will know a life with
You beyond my dreams and business that distract
me. Let Your tenderness overtake me. I ask in the
name of Jesus."

December 17, 2008

Father God – Who do You say that I am?

Me: I come to you Father, and ask ""Who do you say that I am?" – *I watch Moses and say to the Father*, "You listened to his needs." *I take off my shoes.* "I want to know You better and be cared for by You."

Response: "You are a woman of faith. It will continue to grow in you – you are a leader. You will bring great blessings to my people. You are generous, you are gifted for my purposes to be revealed to you later."

"Visit Me more often – continue to rid yourself of things so your environment will be peaceful and clear so that you will have more time for me in a good atmosphere."

January 7, 2009

Jesus, who do You say that I am?

You are a worker in the field for Me

You are tilling the soil to prepare for my coming

You are my friend

You have a good heart and faith

Your mother was right when she said, "You are a woman of substance."

I'm glad your heart is so big to receive Me and others

It's not by chance you found Mother Nadine's teachings

There is still more for you to learn in being a Leader

—a spiritual mother – a nurturer

You are Pat. I love you and am close to you

This is time for more dying to self

My Light shines brightly around you

Your life can bless many

(signed with a heart and a cross)

January 8, 2009

Holy Spirit, Who do you say that I am?

In February, 1974, You were my first, <u>real,</u> powerful encounter with the Trinity. I knew you better than the Father or Jesus, but I had faith in them and Mary.

(Holy Spirit said in my heart): I have been speaking to you and protecting you since you were a little girl.

You are graced to know your neediness <u>but you need</u> to listen to that small inner voice more closely.

You have great inner strength and fortitude and I rejoice when you follow through and obey.

You are loved. You are not to worry about your health. Continue your exercise and diet. I will be with you <u>constantly</u>. You will be healthier than before.

We all love you – you are special.

January 8, 2009

The Stream of Life

Be at peace my cherished ones.

Trust Me my dear ones so you can glide through

life and its obstacles and setbacks and fears

with the fullness of my living waters.

Come to me for this living water that will see

you through your daily life.

Trust Me that I will be your strength, the

undercurrent in this stream of life

wherever you are.

It is I who carry you down the stream of your

daily life.

Stop by the river's edge to refresh yourself

where I may speak to you and teach you of

wisdom and understanding for your life.

My love pours out to you like the waters after

a storm floods the river's bank.

Come and be filled to overflowing everyday

not only when you have trials.

August 16, 2009

Come To Me More Often

Words spoken after reading Song of Songs 2:10-13 in Chapel

"This is a time of change. <u>Come to Me more often. I have much to speak to you about and teach you.</u> Now is the time! <u>Now.</u>

This is the time of your life to give Me your attention. It is time to go with Me in a new direction.

Let the past be behind you with many loving memories. It is a new season of your life – you are Mine. All will be well. Let My waters wash over you and renew you. I have been preparing you!!

You are blossoming and growing and I am calling you. Can you hear Me? Listen!

LISTEN to Me. Come forth my dove, I want to live through you. Let Me hear your voice. I want you to bring My life and healing to others. You can do it with My Light and Love. It is time for a new phase of your life.

I will take care of you and cherish you, My dear one. Do not worry.

I have been pruning you – the old must go to enter into this new place with Me. You can do it – Trust Me with your life.

This will be a time of great happiness and joy for you to overcome any obstacles.

I will entrust many souls to your care. I will be by your side. Warren and Mary Pat and Catherine will be with you. They know Me well."

Me: "I don't know where you're going to take me Lord, but I want to go."

January 14, 2010

Time For Our Restoration

I had just read Zephaniah 3:14-20 and a little earlier Psalm 27:4. I was in a very small chapel on Retreat and talking to our Lord.

"Lord, I do desire to live all my remaining days more consciously aware of your Presence among us and to dwell in your house now – may I remember to gaze, often, on your loveliness and contemplate your temple. Help me to know you more intimately."

Gradually, I could hear in my heart that it was time for my restoration. In my spiritual eyes, interiorly, I see myself amidst throngs, mobs of people in the square in Vatican City below the window where the Pope is seen.

Beneath the window, high on a platform up many steps so all in the rear can see, is a magnificent chair and a person of royalty sitting on the throne. He wears an exquisite crown with glowing jewels, with a red, ruby cross embedded in the front centered in an oval shape.

There is so much light and glow around His Head you can hardly see His features. A sword rests in His right hand and crystal-like globe of the world in His left hand. There were angels all around and more pouring down upon the crowd – beautiful singing.

We are saved and we know it. Each will have a turn, a private audience with Him. We all have scars and wounds from life.

All are patient because we will be with Him – alone – for however long it takes.

My name is called from the crowd – I didn't actually hear it, but knew it was my turn. I walked through an orderly crowd, through the singing and praising and there I was, at the foot of the throne. He stood and said "Come up".

My heart was pounding in awe. He called me, "My dear one. I've been waiting for you."

The power is so strong upon me I have to crawl up the steps sobbing. He reaches His Hand to me and says, "Come up here". I reach for His Hand and He pulls me up the last step or two.

(I knelt/prostrated myself before the Host exposed in the Chapel.)

(me) "In all your glory you are the Risen Christ. He shows me His hands and feet."

(me) "Lord, you didn't respond to all they did to you. I responded poorly and sinfully to many hurts in my life."

He answers me, "That's because I was in touch with my Father every second of the day. You will do better now – your sins have been forgiven. Forgive yourself."

(me) "Please give me the Grace to do that once and for all –"

By now the angels were holding His sword at His right and other angels were holding the World Globe on His left.

He told me to come sit on His lap and His arm was around me – it was quiet, I wasn't hearing any songs or voices from the crowd. I could see the wounds from the crown of thorns – He embraced me and told me, "I would be OK – very good – if the thought of guilt or what I should have done or said ever returned, remember this moment. They should no longer be a part of you or in your mind. You are Mine."

(I drew a Heart with the comment "a blessed visit – Christ on His Throne.")

January 4, 2010

So You Will See the Gift You Are

The old song "You are my special angel sent from above..." comes to mind.

Our Lord speaks to me, "Dear One, empty yourself of all preconceived ideas of who you are, of what you can do and what you cannot do, of how you are perceived or how you are understood. It doesn't matter if someone thinks you're too holy or not holy enough; too good or not good enough; if you're rich or if you're poor; if you are fearful of using some of your gifts or not.

All you need to live and see and understand is how We see you – your Father, My Son and the Holy Spirit. Let all negative thoughts about yourself go and We, We alone, can fill you to overflowing so that you can see yourself as We see you.

So you will see the gift you are and what you can share of your life.

So you will yearn to come and seek us more often

        to hear the beautiful things and the not so

        beautiful things of the world.

So you will be free to learn more and inspire

        others.

So you will be full of our Love and Compassion.

So you will let the Gift of the Spirit flow out.

So you will be filled with discernment, and yes,

So you will love yourself for who you are in Us with

        a grateful heart.

Go and be like Jesus – see yourself as his beloved."

January 28, 2010

"Tell the People I Love Them"

Jonah: 2:8 "When my soul fainted with me, I remember the Lord; my prayer reached you in your holy temple."

Lord, do we have your anointing upon us to begin an evening of prayer ministry?

- "It is time to grow beyond your comfort of Wednesday morning prayer meeting."
- "Stretch yourselves. Bring what you have learned to others in need."
- "Prepare your people well. Many blessings will come of that. I will be with you."
- I am reminded of the song, "Tell the People I love them, tell the People I care."

Psalm 32: 8-11 "I shall instruct you and show you the way you should walk; I will counsel you keeping my eyes on you. But not senseless like horses and mules; with bit and bridle their temper must be curbed. Else they will not come near you."

August 19, 2010

All Will Be Well

"All will be well. This is a time of growth. Listen to me as I draw close."

"Do as the sisters request. I will help you. Do not be anxious. I will be beside you and remind you of my thoughts. I will draw a curtain and you will see more clearly, my Son. This is my work. Do not be worried or want to run away: that is the evil one tempting you to give up. This is the week of Fortitude. Be strong in me. I am with you."

Lord, I feel like I've failed as a leader.

"No, you are bringing souls closer to me. Continue to praise me and worship me."

Lord, I'm worried and concerned about the Core Group. Are we the right ones? Jesus in the Blessed Sacrament have mercy on us.

"The group is right, my daughter. Bear with love and kindness with each one. Be an example so that each can grow deeper in my spirit and become leaders like my apostles did."

I see an image of little pebbles growing into big rocks. "See I am making all things new."

"The Holy Spirit will help each in the core to discern their life so that they can have room for my Son to grow. This is a time to be serious. I will be with each of you so that others in the group can see me in each of you."

September 28, 2010

He Is Calling Us To Listen

We are called to come before our Lord in all our
brokenness and be cleansed by the Blood of the
Lamb.

We are His beloved children and friends being
made whole as he remakes us, molds us and fills us
from His life-giving waters.

He is calling us to listen. Be Silent, Love , Forgive,
be Patient with Gratefulness.
He is washing us clean in His living waters –
purifying us so we can hear Him direct our lives,
our words, to be His witness to mankind.

We are called into silence for His Love to penetrate
any unforgiveness, impatience and any
ungratefulness and sin in our life. Let us turn to
Him and stand in Wonder and Awe so we can hear
His plans for us and how to carry them out.

I see an image of a suffering Christ – a drop of the Precious Blood is upon us. Deliver us from evil. "My desire is wholeness for my people."

The word "LISTEN".

"Speak my words to mankind, make Me known among the nations (through intercessory prayer)." WORDS: prayers like streams of water – IMAGE of stream of water, murky and contaminated. Christ touched it and the water became clean and clear.

Ache and longing – "My heart for My people that they turn to Me. I so long to fill them – turn from your idols….only I can satisfy you. Come to me with your brokenness."

Awesome, awe and wonder and Peace. "I have such plans for you. You will have support."

"Know that I am present with you in your praises, My people, My children. I love you and am anxious to hear and answer your prayers. Speak to me

from your heart not from your needs. He
challenges us to stay on the road to holiness."

2010

My Grace Can Fill Your Soul

Jesus asks, "Tell me, what is it that brings you to

me this day?

As a mother comforts her child, so I will comfort

you.

Speak to me of that which is the greatest need for

you at this time.

Search your heart.

Where is it you struggle most?

My Grace can fill your soul. Listen!

Silence is the discipline by which the inner Fire of

God's love is tended and kept alive. Listen!

Let me lay my hand upon you and heal your

brokenness.

I am the Divine Physician and am doing spiritual

surgery of your body, mind, spirit and soul.

Have faith. You are my beloved one.

Be at Peace – I am in control of your neediness.

Take good care of yourself

and love yourself. I am with you."

October 22, 2013

Come Near to Me and Listen

You are not always aware of my nearness to you at

Mass

Continue my work of loving and healing my people,

teaching them of my great heart filled with many

graces for each

Speak to me – ask!

Be present to me and you shall have your fill as I

prepare you

in the continued work of my redemption of the

world

Contemplate Me

Learn from Me the direction you must go

Speak to me of your needs, sorrows, joys and

gratitude

I wore my crown of thorns for each of you

individually to glorify my father

Come, join me in this work

I love you - I am near

Do not be afraid

No task will be too great for you

October 29, 2013

Turn To Me More Often

I hold you in the palm of my hand

Be filled with My Spirit

Let Me fill you with My Grace

It is yours as my child

Bring My Light to others

Tell them of my Love for them

Be a light for others

You are each so dear to me

I am your Rabboni

Come to me often to refresh you and teach you the

ways of my Spirit

Turn to me more often for My Grace and direction

Listen with your heart to my Voice

Be a gift to others

Bring my love to others

Seek My Presence

You are loved.

November 5, 2013

You Are My Beloved Child

You are my beloved one, you, yes you, I love you.

The Lord lets us know that He is everlasting Love, regardless of what we think about ourselves or our behavior. We can think, I'm not worthy; I'm a sinner; I lack enough faith; I forget that the Holy Spirit resides within me and on and on.

He whispers to us, "You are my beloved child. I was there through the times you were in the darkness, and I was there in the silence of your pain and sadness. I have loved you and have brought you to this time in your life where your heart is ready for more of Me."

"Come away with me, my beloved, into the Light. Experience my warmth, My Peace, My Love, penetrating the core of your body. This is the time to grow in My Love; to grow more deeply into the likeness of Jesus. It is time to live for others."

We are so loved and must come to know and accept that, so that we can share the Light of Christ with those who are in darkness. These are the days which we will commit our life to Christ. These are the days that God has called us, His Beloved, to be filled with His Life so that we can do His work.

The Holy Spirit is seeking our hearts. We need time alone with Him to sit in His Presence. We must have the attitude in our heart that we truly want to walk in His Spirit. When we know that we're beloved, we want to share our life with the one who loves us very much.

Fr. John Powell, S.J. wrote in *Fully Human, Fully Alive*, "We should be living our lives fully alive in the Spirit, using His gifts and reflecting His Presence around us – wherever it is that He sends us. His Light will shine as we yield ourselves to Him. The Light of Christ, hidden in us, will emerge more and more."

January 14, 2014

Be Kind And Merciful

Nurture the little ones in the Spirit

Be kind and merciful as I am

My angels are encamped around my little ones

Who are eager to learn the ways of My Spirit

My angels are hovering over the meetings for

protection of my children

Hearts are opening; minds are open to the Word

These are my special friends (a remnant people?)

Yes, they will be the strong and gifted ones

Pray in earnest for Spiritual protection for them

Their faces will shine with the inner Light of My

Spirit

Do not be anxious, this is My Work

All will be strengthened

March 28, 2014

A Special Prayer for Those Who help the Poor

"My light will come upon you

Blessed are you who take care of my poor ones

Be united in My Spirit for the good of all

Be of one heart and one mind

as this is a great work

Unite together

There will be many graces poured out

upon your work

Open your heart as though it is pierced

as mine was for the love and caring for

your poor brothers and sisters I send to you

Seek after graciousness and humility

I am with you

Respect one another as I speak to each"

June 19, 2014

Heb 10:17 I Have Come To Do Your Will

In prayer, it was as though an angel placed a piece of paper between our Lord's fingers. As I looked at it and wondered about it, it gradually unrolled and became a scroll. I did not know what the message was.

I checked the Concordance about the scroll and read many scriptures listed under scroll. The first one I read was Heb 10:17 "Then I said, 'As is written of me in the book, I have come to do your will, O God.'"

I read many verses from different passages from Jeremiah, Ezk 2:9 and Zech 5:1,2. In some of my reading I came across the word 'fast' and that really tugged at my heart. I cannot say I am good about that at all.

I recalled that in January 2010, on a retreat, there was a prophecy over me by a couple of sisters, "An angel blowing a trumpet with scroll attached and I was sitting with my feet up with a pair of glass slippers on. There was an angel playing a flute – to announce something." I asked, Lord, can you tell me what the angel is announcing to me; what is on the scroll? The answer came back, "It is like it is 11:00 pm and 'not to be announced yet!!!"

Well, Lord, what about those slippers? He answered, "They're the kind Mary wears! Yours are delicate and beautiful like Mary's but very strong like hers. My Mother crushes the serpent's head. You have great inner strength. I want you to use it and remember you have glass slippers like my Mother – a gentle spirit."

Several days later, I asked our Lord, "What is a gentle spirit?" The answer came back, "kindness, love compassion, determination to see a matter through; softness of voice; inner strength without your own power but mine; insightfulness, graceful, beautiful in presentation."

Several days later on that Retreat came these words: "The 'slave drivers' are in your day too – they are those who produce immoral movies, TV, magazines; people who want to control others, wars, greed; growing compulsions in my people tearing them away from goodness and Me – it will get worse until I come. Remember, I can come also through My beloved of faith – My Mother asks for PRAYERS AND FASTING – TAKE HEED."

December 18, 2014

CPSIA information can be obtained
at www.ICGtesting.com
Printed in the USA
FSHW01n0743010818